Kapama

PRIVATE GAME RESERVE

Text:
Ingrid van den Berg

Photography:
Heinrich van den Berg
Philip & Ingrid van den Berg

HPH Publishing

contents

★★★★★
Common name
(Scientific name)

Afrikaans name (A)   German name (G)
French name (F)   Zulu name (Z)

This section gives an indication of the kind of habitat where the animal can be expected and is likely to be found.

It also highlights one or more interesting facts about it. Animals encountered on game drives can be from the entire spectrum of the animal world, but this booklet concentrates on the larger mammal species, only a few small species and some of the common birds that may be seen.

This last section gives even more information, but in a condensed way. Symbols and abbreviations are used and information is in point form.

♀ = female   ♂ = male
☼ = diurnal   ☾ = nocturnal
☼ ☾ = both diurnal and nocturnal
☼(☾) = predominantly diurnal
(☼)☾ = predominantly nocturnal

Please note:
The values for shoulder height, length, mass, gestation and life expectancy can be variable and are meant to give an approximate indication for purposes of comparison.

Indicates in which chapter you are

Sighting rating

★ You will see this animal around every corner.

★ ★ Don't stop too long – you will see it again.

★ ★ ★ Stop and spend some time looking at it.

★ ★ ★ ★ This is an exceptional sighting.

★ ★ ★ ★ ★ Slam on the brakes and get excited.

Chapters

The first section of the book deals with animals that need a lot of space, whether for grazing, browsing or hunting, and are mainly found in larger reserves where one or more of the Big Five are also present. The herbivores are the giants of the African bush and most people find the predators fascinating. Many of the predators are nocturnal but are also encountered throughout the day.

The second section covers animals that are common to most bushveld game reserves. Most of these mammal species are the prey of larger predators and are usually plentiful and often encountered.

The third section covers the less common animals, mainly antelope species. These generally require a very specific kind of habitat, and are mostly regarded as special sightings.

Then there are the animals of the night. Most game reserves do not allow self-drive game viewing at night, but the larger reserves do offer special guided night-drives on open vehicles, which can be very rewarding.

★★★
Giraffe
(Giraffa camelopardalis)

Kameelperd (A)   Giraffe (G)

Girafe (F)   iNdlulamithi (Z)

Look for giraffes where there are food trees for them to browse. They are visible from afar since they are the tallest mammals and the largest ruminants. They have extremely long tongues (45cm) and can reach foliage that is beyond the reach of other browsers. Despite its great length, the giraffe's neck has only seven vertebrae like all other mammals.

Long ago, people thought a giraffe was a cross between a camel, because of the way it walked, and a leopard, because of its markings. This led to the word *camelopardalis*. The Arabs called it Zarafa and the Ethiopians Zurafa. Eventually, taxonomists named it *Giraffa camelopardalis*.

Active: ☼ (☾)   Shoulder height: ♂ 3m ♀ 2.73m
Mass: ♂ 1 192kg ♀ 828kg
Horns: conical outgrowths ♂ more pronounced than ♀
Social structure: loose groups, ♂ often solitary
Collective noun: a corps, herd, tower, stretch, journey, totter or group of giraffes
Gestation: 457 days (15.2 months)
Life expectancy: approximately 28 years

The giants and the killers

★★★★

White Rhinoceros
(Ceratotherium simum)

Witrenoster (A)   Breitmaulnashorn (G)
Rhinocéros blanc (F)   uMkhombe/uBhejane omhlophe (Z)

Look for white rhinos in areas that include grassland with trees, water and mud wallows. They are the second heaviest of all land mammals and spend most of their time grazing. In very hot weather, they may be resting in shade or found wallowing in mud.

There are several ways of distinguishing between the two kinds of rhino. The white rhino has a square upper lip for grazing; pointed, often tufted ears; a flattish back with a slight hump near the middle; an elongated head, which it often holds down; the calf usually runs ahead of the mother; and when alarmed it curls its tail and lifts it above its back.

Active: ☀ ☾
Shoulder height: ♂ 1.8m ♀ 1.7m
Mass: ♂ 2 000kg – 2 400kg ♀ 1 600kg
Horns: two on nose, composed of hair ♂ + ♀
Social structure: solitary and territorial but often in groups
Collective noun: a crash, stubbornness or herd of rhinos
Gestation: 480 days (16 months)
Life expectancy: approximately 45 years

★★★★
African Buffalo
(Syncerus caffer)

Afrika-buffel (A)	Büffel (G)
Buffle d'Afrique (F)	iNyathi (Z)

Buffaloes are often encountered on their way to water after the night feed. They require large space, are bulk grazers and feed on a variety of grasses of various lengths. They prefer open areas, are nomadic and need water every day.

The buffalo lifestyle requires vigilance of all individuals. Females need horns to defend themselves and their offspring against predators, or at least to deter them. They are bovids, which means they have a keratin sheath covering the bone of the horn, making them hollow-horned. These animals are quick-tempered and will not hesitate to use their massive horns to ram and gore if they perceive any threat.

Active: ☀ ☾   Shoulder height: ♂ 1.4m ♀ 1.4m
Mass: ♂ 590kg ♀ 513kg
Horns: ♂ broad base shielding forehead, ♀ bases
not touching
Social structure: non-territorial, large mixed herds,
bachelor herds, and hierarchy structure
Collective noun: a herd, troop, gang or obstinacy of buffaloes
Gestation: 343days (11.5 months)
Life expectancy: approximately 25 years

★ ★ ★ ★

African Savanna Elephant
(Loxodonta africana)

Afrika-olifant (A)　　　　　Afrikanischer elefant (G)
Eléphant d'Afrique (F)　　　　　iNdlovu (Z)

Although they are Earth's largest land animals, they blend perfectly into the bush and can easily be passed by unnoticed. The trunk is the muscular extension of the upper lip, containing the nostrils and two fingerlike projections. They are strict vegetarians and feed on bark, roots, leaves, soft branches, grass and fruit.

When elephants approach, give them space to pass, switch off the engine and keep calm. Elephants may try to scare off intruders by kicking up dust, flapping ears, 'bush bashing', trumpeting and lifting the trunk – actions all intended to intimidate. Serious charges are silent, with ears pinned back and trunk lowered.

Active: ☀ ☾　　　Shoulder height: ♂ 3.45m ♀ 2.62m
Mass: ♂ 5 500kg – 6 000kg ♀ 4 000kg
♂ + ♀ with tusks, absence usually genetic
Social structure: matriarchal clan, ♂ alone or bachelor herds
Collective noun: a herd, memory or parade of elephants
Gestation: 22 months (88 weeks)
Life expectancy: approximately 60 years

The giants and the killers

Hippopotamus
(Hippopotamus amphibius)

Seekoei (A)   Grossflusspferd (G)

Hippopotame (F)   iMvubu (Z)

Look for hippos resting in water or basking on the bank close to their waterhole during the day. They usually have their preferred places. The water must be deep enough to cover their bodies and prevent them from overheating. At night they are lone grazers, and consume up to 40kg per adult.

Although hippos in Africa kill more people than lions or crocodiles do, they are only dangerous when they feel threatened or their space is invaded. Their agility and speed must never be underestimated as they can run faster than humans. A threat display of yawning, showing their long razor-sharp canines, usually discourages aggressors.

Active: (☼) in water   ☾ grazing

Shoulder height: ♂ 1.5m ♀ 1.44m

Mass: ♂ 1 546kg ♀ 1 385kg

♂ lower canine 22cm ♀ 14cm

Social structure: sociable groups of a ♂ and many ♀'s

Collective noun: a crash, herd, raft, pod, thunder, school, bloat or huddle of hippos

Gestation: 225 – 257 days (8 months)

Life expectancy: approximately 54 years

★ ★ ★ ★ ★

Cheetah
(Acinonyx jubatus)

Jagluiperd (A)   Gepard (G)

Guépard (F)   iNgulule (Z)

The cheetah needs bushes, grass or other cover to get within sprinting range of its prey. It is built for speed – light-boned, long thin-legged, short necked, with a slender body and a long tail. It can attain a speed of up to 100km per hour, making it the fastest mammal on land.

The unsheathed claws are less retractile than those of other cats, so that the claws stay out to give the cheetah grip when chasing prey. Their bird-like chirp or whistling call is unlike that of any of the other cats.

Active: ☼
Shoulder height: ♂ 90cm ♀ 75cm
Mass: ♂ 65kg ♀ 35kg
♂ + ♀ similar in appearance
Social structure: breeding ♂ territorial, often has a coalition partner
Collective noun: a coalition of cheetahs
Gestation: 90 – 98 days (3 months)
Life expectancy: approximately 15 years
Enemies: lion, leopard and hyena will kill its young and chase it off its prey

18

Black-backed Jackal
(Canis mesomelas)

Rooijakkals/Swartrugjakkals (A)   Schabrackenschakal (G)
Chacal à chabraque (F)   iMpungushe (Z)

The black-backed jackal is widely distributed and not very popular with farmers because it may kill small livestock such as sheep and goats. The saddle of black and silver hair is very characteristic and distinguishes it from the side-striped jackal, which is very shy and seldom seen.

A jackal pair forms a partner bond for life and an individual will only find another mate should one partner die. Both sexes mark and defend a territory and help to raise the young. The mated pair often forages together or shares food when foraging singly.

Active: (☼) ☾
Shoulder height: 38cm
Mass: ♂ 8kg ♀ 7.4kg
Social structure: only one partner, pair bond and territorial
Collective noun: a skulk of jackals
Gestation: 60 – 65 days (2 months)
Life expectancy: approximately 10 years
Enemies: lion, leopard and large birds of prey

Spotted Hyena
(Crocuta crocuta)

Gevlekte hiëna (A)   Flecken hyäne (G)

Hyène tachetée (F)   iMpisi (Z)

This sturdily-built, large, formidable scavenger and predator is often encountered early in the morning, walking along the road returning to its den. The clan is a matriarchal society with the dominant and other females being larger than the males. It is untrue that these animals are bisexual, but a flap of skin that resembles the male organ covers the reproductive tract of the female.

Hyenas serve a vital purpose in the ecology of an area because they help to clear the bush of decomposing carcasses, and prey on dying or infirm animals. This helps to maintain healthy animal populations.

Active: (☼) ☾

Shoulder height: ♂ 80.2cm ♀ 79.4cm

Mass: ♂ 62.5kg ♀ 68.2kg

♂ smaller than ♀

Social structure: matriarchal clan system with rank order

Collective noun: a clan or cackle of hyenas

Gestation: 110 days (4 months)

Life expectancy: approximately 20 – 25 years

Enemies: lion but also leopard and wild dog

★ ★ ★ ★
Lion
(Panthera leo)

Leeu (A)   Löwe (G)
Lion d'Afrique (F)   iBhubesi (Z)

Lions have no specific habitat preference and can be encountered anywhere, except in forests. In the early morning they often rest on the road or are found on a kill. Different prides have different hunting preferences and patterns. The commonest prey is impala, zebra and wildebeest, but some prides regularly kill buffalo and giraffe, and will also take a variety of small prey, or even scavenge like hyenas.

In a lion pride, all the females will be related and the cubs and sub-adults will have been fathered by the male coalition in control of the pride. When a new male coalition takes over a pride, they usually kill all the cubs of the previous males, so that the females can come on heat sooner to bear the new coalition's own offspring.

Active: (☼) ☽   Shoulder height: 1.2m
Mass: ♂ 190kg – 200kg ♀ 126kg
♂ with mane appearing in 3rd year
Social structure: pride related ♀'s and brotherhood ♂'s, social
Collective noun: a pride, sault, troop, or sowse of lions
Gestation: 105 days (3.5 months)
Life expectancy: approximately 20 years

Leopard
(Panthera pardus)

Luiperd (A)   Leopard (G)
Panthère/Léopard (F)   iNgwe (Z)

Although well represented in places, its shy secretive ways and mainly nocturnal habits are reasons for it being only rarely sighted. This is the most widespread of all predators since it has the broadest habitat tolerance of all. Beautiful, powerful and stealthy, it surely is the prize encounter on all game drives.

The leopard's method of hunting is stalking and then pouncing on to the prey, taking it by surprise. The large head and neck are essential for holding and subduing the kill, which is often hoisted up a tree to get it out of reach of other predators.

Active: (☀) ☾
Shoulder height: ♂ 77cm ♀ 66cm
Mass: ♂ 63kg ♀ 37kg
♂ bigger and heavier than ♀
Social structure: solitary, territorial
Collective noun: a leap, leep or lepe of leopards
Gestation: 106 days (3.4 months)
Life expectancy: approximately 20 years
Enemies: lion, wild dog, hyena

Crocodile
(Crocodylus niloticus)

Krokodil (A)   Krokodil (G)
Crocodile (F)   iNgwenya (Z)

Crocodiles are reptiles and easy to see when sunning themselves on riverbanks. They are cold-blooded and need to absorb heat from the sun. Their ability to lie concealed with most of their body underwater, combined with their speed over short distances, makes them effective opportunistic hunters of larger prey. They grab such prey in their powerful jaws, drag it into the water, and hold it under until it drowns.

Eggs are laid in sand on sunny riverbanks and are incubated by the sun. The sex of the hatchlings depends on the incubation temperature; females are produced at low temperatures and males at higher temperatures.

Active: ☀ basking in sun ☾ under water
Snout to tail end: ♂ 2.5m – 3.9m (can be up to 6m)
Mass: ♂ 450kg – 600kg
Amphibious, communal, parents look after nests
Collective noun: a congregation, float, bask or nest of crocodiles
Gestation: 16 – 80 eggs are laid and hatch within 85 days
Life expectancy: approximately 45 years

Plains Zebra
(Equus quagga)

Bontsebra (A)   Steppenzebra (G)
Zèbre de Burchell (F)   iDube (Z)

Look for zebras on grasslands, plains and open or lightly wooded areas, close to water. The males and females look alike and are often found in large aggregations at water holes. Note that the lower legs and belly have no stripes and that shadow stripes occur between the black stripes. No two zebras have exactly the same stripe pattern.

Zebras often rest in pairs with their heads placed on the other's back, facing in opposite directions. This enables a pair to watch for danger in all directions and brush flies off each other's face.

Active: ☀ ☾
Shoulder height: ♂ 1.3m ♀ 1.3m
Mass: ♂ 313kg ♀ 302kg
Social structure: gregarious, non-territorial, small family groups
Collective noun: a zeal, cohort, dazzle or herd of zebras
Gestation: 360 – 390 days (12 – 13 months)
Life expectancy: approximately 35 years
Enemies: lion, but also hyena and wild dog

Common bushveld animals

★

Blue Wildebeest

(Connochaetes taurinus)

Blouwildebees (A) Streifengnu (G)
Gnou bleu/à queue noire (F) iNkonkoni (Z)

You will find these animals in small or large herds on short-grass plains and acacia savanna. The blue wildebeests, with their blunt muzzles and wide row of incisors, prefer short grasses. Unfortunately, they cannot reach these unless they are exposed and therefore they are often seen following zebras who graze medium-height grasses, exposing the short grasses.

Scent-marking is important for territorial species such as wildebeest. The pre-orbital gland is situated between the eye and the nose, and is rubbed against twigs, stems, grass stalks or trees to communicate by scent with other members of the species.

Active: ☼ ☾
Shoulder height: ♂ 1.74m ♀ 1.35m
Mass: ♂ 249.8kg ♀ 182.7kg
Horns: ♂ well developed bosses, ♀ lighter in build
Social structure: gregarious, big herds, territorial ♂, ♀ herds, bachelor groups
Collective noun: a herd or implausibility of wildebeests
Gestation: 250 days (8.4 months)

★

Impala

(Aepyceros melampus)

Rooibok (A)

Impala/Schwarzfersenantilope (G)

Impala (F)

iMpala (Z)

Impalas will probably be the first game species you encounter on your visit – they are abundant and by far the commonest animals in bushveld reserves. They are grazers and/or browsers, depending on the habitat, but prefer open woodland.

The black tufts on the rear feet above the hooves are scent glands. Adult males also have scent glands on the face, which the dominant males often use to mark their territories and advertise their presence by rubbing scent on to the trunks of trees and other vegetation. During the rutting season there is much roaring and aggression amongst the males as they fight for dominance.

Active: ☀   Shoulder height: ♂ 90cm ♀ 89cm
Mass: ♂ 44kg ♀ 40kg
Horns: only ♂
Social structure: territorial ♂ + breeding herd;
bachelor herd
Collective noun: a herd or rank of impalas
Gestation: 196 days (6.5 months)
Life expectancy: unknown

★★

Greater Kudu
(Tragelaphus strepsiceros)

Koedoe (A)	Kudu (G)
Koudou (F)	uMgankla/iMbodwane (Z)

Kudus are found in places where there is dense cover, such as scrubby woodland. They prefer rocky, broken terrain. They are browsers and are well concealed by their colouring. The males of this second-tallest of antelope have the most spectacular horns, while the smaller females are hornless. They display the huge cupped ears of the species to best advantage.

Despite being long and twisted, the horns never get in the way when the antelope flees from predators – it simply lifts its chin so that the horns lie flat at shoulder level. They are high jumpers, clearing fences up to 2.5m high.

Active: ☀ ☾
Shoulder height: 1.45m
Mass: ♂ 220kg ♀ 152kg
Horns: only ♂ corkscrew twisted, long
Social structure: gregarious, small herds
Collective noun: a cluster or herd of kudus
Gestation: 270 days (9 months)
Life expectancy: approximately 11 years
Enemies: leopard, wild dog, cheetah and lion

Common bushveld animals

Common/Grey Duiker

(Sylvicapra grimmia)

Gewone duiker (A)
Kronenducker (G)

Céphalophe couronné (F)
iMpunzi (Z)

Look for duikers in areas with ample shrubs and other plants growing under trees. This is one of the most common small antelope in the bushveld and the last to be eliminated by settlements. Its diet is varied but it eats mainly herbs, fruits, seeds and cultivated crops.

They are secretive and, if disturbed, will steal away with head lowered and tail up. When they suddenly decide to flee, they seem to dash between hiding places, almost diving into thickets. *'Duiker'* is the Afrikaans word for diver. Both sexes have a characteristic spiky tuft of hair between the ears.

Active: ☼ ☾   Shoulder height: 50cm
Mass: ♂ 16.2kg ♀ 16.7kg
Horns: ♂ short and straight, ♀ absent or stunted
Social structure: usually solitary
Collective noun: a pair of duikers
Gestation: 191 days (6.3 months)
Life expectancy: approximately 9 years
Enemies: Many, including large and smaller predators, crocodile, python and large birds of prey

Steenbok/Steinbuck
(Raphicerus campestris)

Steenbok (A)   Steinböckchen (G)
Steenbok (F)   iQhina (Z)

This tiny antelope is common in the open and dry bush-veld. It is not dependent on water sources, since it obtains sufficient moisture from its diet of foliage, seedpods and seeds, berries and tender green grass. Sexes are alike, except for the horns.

Both sexes are territorial and defend their areas against others. They use dung middens. When about to urinate or defecate, the antelope prepares a slight depression with its front hooves, in which it leaves a deposit and then covers it up. When they sense danger, they hide in the grass by lying flat to escape detection, not moving unless they are flushed out.

Active: ☀ ☾
Shoulder height: 50cm
Mass: ♂ 10.9kg ♀ 11.3kg
Horns: only ♂ short and straight
Social structure: solitary, territorial
Collective noun: a pair of steenbokke/steinbucks
Gestation: 168 – 173 days (5.6 months)
Life expectancy: approximately 9 years

40

Common Warthog
(Phacochoerus africanus)

Vlakvark (A)   Warzenschwein (G)

Phacochère (F)   iNtibane (Z)

Look for warthogs on floodplains, open areas, dry pans and around waterholes. They avoid dense cover and favour open short grassland with edible grasses, rhizomes, bulbs and tubers. Warthogs often drop down on the knees of their forelegs to dig more effectively, using their snouts. They do not depend on water sources, but nevertheless drink fairly regularly and enjoy mud-wallowing.

The warthog's foremost enemies are the lion and leopard. They defend themselves with their long canines called tushes. The lower ones are razor sharp and slightly curved but shorter than the upper ones, against which they are honed when the animal eats.

Active: ☼   Shoulder height: ♂ 68cm ♀ 60cm

Mass: ♂ 79kg ♀ 66kg

Warts: ♂ 2 pairs of warts on face, ♀ one pair

Social structure: sows live in clans with young, no territorialism

Collective noun: a sounder or clan of warthogs

Gestation: 164 – 182 days (5.5 – 6 months)

Life expectancy: approximately 20 years

Vervet Monkey
(Cercophitecus pygerythrus)

Blou-aap (A)   Grünmeerkatze (G)
Vervet (F)   iNkawu (Z)

Monkeys are often found in vegetation close to streams or rivers. They live in troops of family groups, favouring areas with trees for shelter, and eat mostly plant material. They also eat insects, lizards, birds' eggs and nestlings.

The troop has a dominant male that maintains his status with grimacing and threatening gestures. Grooming is a way of cleaning and neatening the fur, getting rid of big ticks, scabs, flakes of skin and salty deposits caused by perspiration. But the activity is also a way of building bonds and alliances between individuals, and reinforcing hierarchies.

Active: ☼   Snout to tail end: ♂ 114cm ♀ 102cm
Mass: ♂ 5.5kg ♀ 4kg
♂ with vivid genital colouring
Social structure: gregarious with a clear order of dominance within the troop
Collective noun: a shrewdness, cartload, tribe, troup or troop of monkeys
Gestation: 165 days (5.5 months)
Life expectancy: approximately 30 years

★

Chacma Baboon
(Papio ursinus)

Bobbejaan (A)   Tchakmapavian/Bärenpavianaffe (G)
Le Chacma (F)   iMfene (Z)

This species occurs throughout southern Africa's bushveld areas, wherever there is water and secure sleeping places. Baboons are often seen as the troop moves from its sleeping tree to foraging grounds. They eat almost anything – grasses, seeds, flowers, fruits, tubers and bulbs, insects, frogs, reptiles, eggs and even small mammals.

When a troop is feeding or on the move, certain individuals, usually males, will climb on to vantage points from where they scan the environment for potential danger. Loud barking is usually an alarm call that warns the troop of danger. These lookouts also help to protect the juveniles by keeping them from straying.

Active: ☼   Shoulder height: 75cm
Mass: ♂ 22kg – 32kg ♀ 14kg – 16kg
Social structure: live in mixed troops and have a complex society
Collective noun: a flange, troup, troop, tribe, congress or rumpus of baboons
Gestation: 183 days (6 months)
Life expectancy: approximately 30 – 45 years

46

★★

Slender Mongoose
(Galerella sanguinea)

Swartkwasmuishond (A)   Schlankemanguste (G)
Mangouste rouge (F)   uChakide (Z)

This mongoose is usually seen alone and is only noticed when alarmed or when crossing the road. It can easily be confused with the dwarf mongoose, but is larger and the long tail is black-tufted. It is very common and widely distributed in woodlands and wooded savanna and feeds on small vertebrates and insects.

They show an unusual social organisation in that adult

males usually live in coalitions of up to four males – very much like the coalitions of lion and cheetah males. They defend a collective territory that may include several females. When they forage, they do so alone.

Active: ☼
Snout to tail end: 32cm
Mass: ♂ 715g ♀ 575g
Social structure: coalition males defend a territory with a few ♀
Collective noun: a business of mongooses
Gestation: 56 – 63 days (2 months)
Life expectancy: approximately 15 years

Banded Mongoose
(Mungos mungo)

Gebande muishond (A)   Zebramanguste (G)
Mangue raye'e (F)   uBuhala/uBuhaye (Z)

The first sighting of the banded mongoose is often one of disbelief – especially when they approach in a closed pack of fast moving, wriggling little brown banded bodies, heads low to the ground. They are widely distributed and quite common in the bushveld where they prey on invertebrates and occasionally also on larger vertebrates like rodents and snakes. They often pay visits to camps and lodges where they scavenge on garbage.

Banded mongooses can intimidate predators the size of serval and jackal with mob attacks. They have strong social bonds, which they reinforce by social grooming and vocal signals. Scent marking is another ritual in marking their territories.

Their enemies include raptors, African wild cat, serval, jackal and badger.

Active: ☼
Snout to tail end: 33cm – 41cm
Mass: 1kg – 2kg
Social structure: up to 35 in pack, includes 3–4 breeding ♀'s
Collective noun: a business of mongooses
Gestation: 56 – 63 days (2 months)
Life expectancy: approximately 13 years

Dwarf Mongoose
(Helogale parvula)

Dwergmuishond (A)
Mangouste nain (F)

Zwergigneumon (G)
uChakide (Z)

Dwarf mongooses are some of the commonest carnivores in Africa. In the early morning, as they leave their den, they first socialise and sun themselves before they start foraging for the day. The dens are often in old termite mounds, hollow trees or crevices. They live in packs of up to nine adult individuals and many young.

Only the dominant individuals of the pack breed and the rest of the pack, who are mostly related, help to raise the young. Females without young are also able to produce milk to help with nursing, even though they have never been pregnant.

Active:
Snout to tail end: 24cm
Mass: ♂ 350g – 400g
Social structure: live in packs with one breeding pair, cooperative rearing of young
Collective noun: a business of mongooses
Gestation: 63 days (2 months)
Life expectancy: approximately 10 years
Enemies: raptors, African wild cat, serval, jackal, badger

Tree Squirrel
(Paraxerus cepapi)

Boomeekhoring (A)   Baumhörnchen (G)
L'écureuils des bois (F)   yaSezihlahleni (Z)

The tree squirrel is widespread but occurs mainly in well developed woodland regions, e.g. Mopane savanna.

Although usually a solitary rodent, the tree squirrel may occur in family groups during the breeding season and is often first noticed when mobbing an intruder by making a loud chucking sound, while flicking its bushy tail over its body. Groups can also sometimes be seen in the morning huddled together in the forks of trees, grooming and sunning themselves. It forages on the ground, but when disturbed it tends to head for the nesting hole, which may mean scurrying up a tree and leaping from tree to tree.

Active: ☀
Snout to tail end: 35cm (half of this is the tail)
Mass: 200g
Social structure: territorial family groups
Collective noun: a dray of squirrels
Gestation: 56 days (1.8 months)
Life expectancy: approximately 15 years
Enemies: mongoose, caracal, genet, raptors, python

Common bushveld animals

★★

Bushbuck

(Tragelaphus scriptus)

Bosbok (A)   Buschbock/Schirrantilope (G)

Antilope harnaché/Guib (F)   uNkonka (Z)

Look for the bushbuck along forest edges and densely vegetated places near water. It occurs more widely than the Nyala, but also prefers the same kind of habitat. It browses, but also feeds on seeds, fruits, flowers and tender green grass.

This solitary antelope is neither territorial, nor does it defend its home range. The stripes and spots on its coat help with camouflage, blending it perfectly with the dappled shade of its surroundings. Cornered bushbuck males can be extremely dangerous, using their sharp horns and hooves to good effect. An enraged bushbuck can even scare off leopard.

Active: (☼) ☾
Shoulder height: ♂ 79cm ♀ 69cm
Mass: ♂ 40kg – 80kg ♀ 50kg – 60kg
Horns: only ♂ with twisted horns
Social structure: ♂ solitary ♀ solitary or with a young
Collective noun: a cluster of bushbucks
Gestation: 180 days (6 months)
Life expectancy: approximately 9 years

56

Animals of specific habitats

★★★

Nyala
(Tragelaphus angasii)

Njala (A)   Tieflandnyala (G)
Nyala (F)   iNyala (Z)

Nyalas are common only in the Zululand bushveld and the
north-eastern parts of southern Africa. You will find this
close relative of the bushbuck in thickets and dense woodland, generally near water. It browses on leaves, feeds on
pods, fruits, herbs and also on fresh green grass.

The colour of the male coat differs considerably from
that of the female, and becomes darker as it matures. The
dominance display of a male is spectacular – it struts with
mane erect and neck arched, and presents its flank to the
rival, making itself appear bigger. The tail is raised over
the rump and the white hairs fan out; the head is lowered
and the horns point outward.

Active: (☼) ☾   Shoulder height: 106cm
Mass: ♂ 106kg ♀ 60kg
Horns: only ♂ with twisted horns
Social structure: gregarious, not territorial,
♀ with last few offspring, ♂ in small groups
Collective noun: a cluster of nyalas
Gestation: 220 days (7 months)
Life expectancy: approximately 9 years

Animals of specific habitats

Waterbuck
(Kobus ellipsiprymnus)

Waterbok/Kringgat (A)　　　　　　Wasserbock (G)

Cobe à croissant (F)　　　　　　　　iPhiva (Z)

Look for waterbucks in grassland at the edges of savanna woodland, close to wetlands and water. It is a grazer of medium and short grasses and browses on foliage when green grass is not available.

The white ring around the rump probably serves as a following mechanism – each animal follows the signal of the animal in front, and in turn serves as a following beacon for the one behind. Abundant sweat glands secrete a musky substance, which taints the flesh and gives it an unpleasant flavour that effectively deters predators and other hunters.

Active: ☀ ☾　　　Shoulder height: 1.3m

Mass: ♂ 270kg ♀ 250kg

Horns: only ♂, large, slightly but sweepingly curled forward

Social structure: social and occur in groups, dominant males territorial

Collective noun: a herd or cluster of waterbucks

Gestation: 280 days (8.5 – 9 months)

Life expectancy: approximately 12 years

Southern Reedbuck

(Redunca arundinum)

Rietbok (A)
Redunca grande (F)

Großriedbock (G)
uMziki (Z)

Reedbucks can be found where there are stands of high grass or reedbeds near water. They depend on the existence of wetlands, vleis and seasonally moist grasslands.

Reedbucks have a distinctive voice. When disturbed they give a characteristic piercing whistle and run in a distinctive rocking canter, displaying their white tail, and whistling at every bound. The clicking sound is caused by forced expulsion of breath through the nostrils, varying in pitch and tone. In distress, the voice is a long-drawn plaintive cry, but when suddenly frightened, it makes a soft hissing sound.

Active: (☼) ☾
Shoulder height: ♂ 0.9m ♀ 0.8m
Mass: ♂ 70kg ♀ 51kg
Horns: only ♂
Social structure: not gregarious but form pairs or family groups
Collective noun: a cluster or pair of reedbucks
Gestation: 225 days (8 months)
Life expectancy: approximately 9 years

Porcupine

(Hystrix africaeaustralis)

Ystervark (A)	Süd-Afrika stachelschwein (G)
Porc-épique sud-Africain (F)	iNgungubane/iNzenga (Z)

Look out for porcupines on night drives and in wooded areas where they may be seen feeding on the bark of trees, roots or bulbs. The back and hindquarters of this large rodent are protected by pliable spines, hard sharp quills, and flattened bristly hairs.

It is untrue that porcupines shoot their quills. When approached by a predator, they may rattle their quills, run backwards or sideways into the aggressor causing the sharp quills to penetrate the skin and frighten it away. The quills are modified hairs, hollow and robust, and are banded in white and black, the classic nocturnal warning colours.

Active: ☾
Snout to tail end: ♂ 100cm ♀ 73cm
Mass: ♂ 11.5kg ♀ 13.7kg
♂ + ♀ similar
Social structure: found singly or in pairs,
mate for life, territorial
Collective noun: a pair of porcupines
Gestation: 93 – 94 days (3 months)
Life expectancy: approximately 15 – 20 years

Ground Pangolin

(Manis temminckii)

Ietermagog (A)   Steppenschuppentier (G)
Pangolin de Temminck (F)

Look for pangolins on floodplain grasslands and rocky slopes where the soil is sandy. They feed mainly on ants and termites, using the claws on their forefeet to open underground food sources, and lick up ants and termites with their long sticky tongue. Pangolins have no teeth and the food is ground up in the muscular part of the stomach, aided by grit.

   Pangolins are armoured with heavy yellow-brown scales and walk on their hind legs with the tail off the ground, forelegs and head just above the ground. They defend themselves simply by rolling into a ball when threatened and are seldom preyed upon.

Active: (☼) ☾
Snout to tail end: ♂ 1m ♀ 0.9m
Mass: ♂ 13.3kg ♀ 7.4kg
♂ + ♀ similar in appearance
Social structure: solitary
Collective noun: a pair of pangolins
Gestation: 139 days (4.7 months)
Life expectancy: approximately 12 years

Creatures of the night

★ ★ ★ ★ ★

Bushpig
(Potamochoerus larvatus)

Bosvark (A)

Potamochère (F)

Buschschwein (G)

iNgulube (Z)

Look out for bushpigs in riverine vegetation where there are dense thickets or tall grass for cover. They are shy and highly nocturnal animals, seldom seen during the day. They eat virtually anything from plant matter, insects and worms, and occasionally even feed on carrion.

Bushpigs do not drop to their knees when rooting plants as warthogs do, nor do they have warts. Unlike warthogs, they run with their tails down, and their tushes (tusks) are inconspicuous. Like warthogs, they enjoy mud-wallowing, probably to get rid of insects and for temperature control. They are aggressive and dangerous and their sharp tusks can inflict serious wounds.

Active: (☀) ☾
Shoulder height: 70cm
Mass: ♂ 72kg ♀ 68kg
Social structure: only one partner,
gregarious but not territorial
Collective noun: a sounder of bushpigs
Gestation: 119 days (4 months)
Life expectancy: approximately 20 years

★ ★ ★ ★ ★

Aardvark/Antbear
(Orycteropus afer)

Erdvark (A) Erdferkel (G)
Oryctérope (F)

The aardvark only starts foraging late at night and is therefore seldom seen on drives. Although these animals have pig-like snouts, they are not related to pigs at all. They use their powerful forelegs to excavate burrows where they live, and also to excavate the nests of formicid ants and, to a lesser extent, termites.

The aardvark locates its food source by its acute sense of smell complemented by a good sense of hearing. Their large ears are movable and help to detect movement and the presence of danger. Their eyesight, however, is very poor.

Active: (☼) ☾
Snout to tail end: ♂ 1.7m ♀ 1.5m
Mass: ♂ 45kg ♀ 41kg
Social structure: solitary
Collective noun: an aarmoury of aardvarks
Gestation: 243 days (8 months)
Life expectancy: approximately 10 years
Enemies: all big predators, python

Lesser Galago/Bushbaby
(Galago moholi)

Nagapie (A)   Kleiner galago (G)
Peu de bushbaby (F)

Look for this tiny primate in woodland with typical acacia stands. Acacias are a source of gum and have a rich insect life, both important food items for the bushbaby. Its eyes are noticeably large in relation to the head.

It lives in the dense canopies of trees, resting during the day in groups of up to six on a platform-like nest. It sleeps curled up on its side, covered by its tail. It is extremely agile and able to leap a few metres at a time. On the ground it hops, using its hind legs only.

Active: ☾
Snout to tail end: 37cm
Mass: ♂ 165g ♀ 150g
Social structure: small groups
Collective noun: a group of galagos
Gestation: 121 – 124 days (4 months)
Life expectancy: approximately 14 years
Enemies: nocturnal raptors, genet and python

★★★★

Thick-tailed Bushbaby

(Otolemur crassicaudatus)

Bosnagaap (A)

Bushbaby épais-coupé la queue (F)

Riesengalago (G)

siNkwe (Z)

This animal is associated with well-developed woodland where there is tree gum to be found. It is often heard in rest camps at night. Its raucous, crow-like cries attract attention, not only from their own companions, but also from rivals. It rests in nests in trees during the day and emerges after sunset, first to groom and then to forage.

Their eyes are smaller in relation to their head size than the lesser galago, but also shine brightly in the darkness with a reddish glow if they are caught in a beam of light. They run along branches, with short jumps where necessary. On the ground they move on all fours with hindquarters and the tail held high.

Active: ☾
Snout to tail end: ♂ 71cm ♀ 58cm
Mass: ♂ 1.2kg ♀ 0.74kg
Social structure: stable groups
Collective noun: a group of galagos
Gestation: 132 – 135 days (more than 4 months)
Life expectancy: approximately 15 years
Enemies: nocturnal raptors, genet and python

★ ★ ★ ★ ★

Honey Badger
(Mellivora capensis)

Ratel (A)   Honigdachs (G)
Ratel (F)

Although badgers are mainly nocturnal, they are often encountered during the day. This is a very tough and fear-less predator that will attack any other animal it perceives as a threat, even a lion. They feed on insects, spiders, reptiles, birds, mice and rats and will unearth any prey with their powerful forelimbs, which are adapted for digging.

Badgers are also particularly fond of honey and bee larvae. The predation on bees and its association with the greater honey guide is particularly fascinating. The bird regularly invites people and other animals such as badgers, to follow it to the nearest bee-hive. The co-operation offers mutual benefits.

Active: (☼) ☾
Snout to tail end: 95cm
Mass: ♂ + ♀ 12kg
Social structure: only one partner, pair bond
Collective noun: a cete or colony of badgers
Gestation: 50 – 70 days (2 months)
Life expectancy: approximately 24 years

★★★★★

Caracal/Desert Lynx
(Caracal caracal)

Rooikat (A)

Caracal (F)

Wüstenluchs/Caracal (G)

iNdabushe (Z)

A sighting of caracal in the wild is always a special one. Being shy, well camouflaged and nocturnal, it is not often seen, although it is plentiful. It inhabits plains, mountains and rocky hills, and seems to need woody vegetation for cover. A good climber and jumper, it is an awesome predator, often killing prey much larger than itself.

This is the heaviest of the small cats and is the African version of the lynx. The tufts at the ends of the ears are distinctive and probably serve to accentuate the ears in interaction with other individuals. In farming areas, it is regarded as a problem animal.

Active: (☀) ☾
Shoulder height: ♂ 48cm ♀ 43cm
Mass: ♂ 13kg ♀ 10kg
Social structure: solitary and territorial
Collective noun: a pair of caracals
Gestation: 62 – 81 days (between 2 and 3 months)
Life expectancy: approximately 12 years
Enemies: man

★★★★

African Wild Cat
(Felis silvestris)

Vaalboskat (A)

Chat ganté (F)

Wildkatze (G)

iMpaka (Z)

Expect to see the African wild cat wherever mice and rats thrive – perhaps even close to lodges and in camps. When other predators are abundant, sightings will occur strictly at night. Occasionally you may find an African wild cat early morning on its way to its resting place, or sunning itself.

This is the closest relative to the domestic tabby and can easily be mistaken for it. Its long legs, bright rufous-brown, orange to chestnut markings on the back of its ears and its more upright posture when sitting, distinguish it from its domestic counterpart.

Active: ☾

Snout to tail end: ♂ 92cm ♀ 88cm

Mass: ♂ 5.1kg ♀ 4.2kg

Social structure: solitary

Collective noun: a destruction, dowt or dout of wild cats

Gestation: 65 days (2 months)

Life expectancy: approximately 12 – 18 years

Enemies: leopard and other predators

★★★★★
Serval
(Leptailurus serval)

Tierboskat (A)   Servalkatze (G)
Serval/Chat-tigre (F)   iNdlozi (Z)

The best place to see servals is along wetlands where there is tall grass for cover and plenty of rodents for food. They start foraging in the early evening, and are often still active after sunrise. It is the tallest of the small African cats, has long legs and is slenderly built with a long neck.

It is exceptionally quick and agile, and captures its prey by pouncing – first locating and pinpointing the sound made by its prey by moving its large ears, listening, and then leaping high in the air and coming down with both front feet on its victim. Prey includes mainly rats and mice, but also other rodents, reptiles, birds and mammals.

Active: (☀) ☾
Shoulder height: 60cm
Mass: ♂ 11kg ♀ 9.6kg
Social structure: exclusive core territories
Collective noun: a pair of servals
Gestation: 73 days (2.4 months)
Life expectancy: approximately 12 – 17 years
Enemies: larger predators

★★★★

Large-spotted Genet
(Genetta tigrina)

Grootkolmuskejaatkat (A)   Grossfleck ginsterkatze (G)

Genetta à grandes taches/Genette tigrine (F)   iNsimba (Z)

During night drives, look for the large-spotted genet on the ground or in trees of densely wooded areas close to water. This genet only occurs in the higher rainfall areas and can be distinguished by the black-tipped tail. It hunts in trees and on the ground and eats rodents, insects, birds and wild fruit.

Females give birth to litters of up to three in holes or in leaf nests. When moving them, the mother carries them by the back, not the nape of the neck as other cats do. Genets are closely related to mongooses.

Active: ☾
Snout to tail end: 95cm
Mass: ♂ 1.8kg ♀ 1.7kg
Social structure: solitary
Collective noun: a pair of genets
Gestation: 70 – 77 days (2.6 months)
Life expectancy: approximately 9 – 10 years
Enemies: serval, caracal, leopard, badger, nocturnal raptors

★ ★ ★ ★ ★

African Civet
(Civettictis civetta)

Siwet (A)   Afrika zibetkatze (G)

Civett d'Afrique (F)   iGaga (Z)

This large, striking but secretive relative of the genet is very common in the bushveld but only occasionally seen. Its habit of scavenging attracts it to places like camps and lodges where it prowls around at night, often overturning rubbish bins.

This is the only predator that seems to thrive on eating unpleasant tasting or even toxic millipedes and toads. They even consume poisonous snakes like the puffadder, but they also scavenge and supplement their diet with a variety of fruit. The musk secreted as a territorial marking has been used in the past as an ingredient of perfume.

Active: ☾

Snout to tail end: ♂ 1m – 1.5m

Mass: ♂ + ♀ 16kg – 20kg

Social structure: solitary

Collective noun: a pair of civets

Gestation: about 80 days (2.7 months)

Life expectancy: approximately 15 years

Enemies: leopard and caracal, other small predators, python and raptors

Creatures of the night

★
Scrub Hare
(Lepus saxatilis)

Kolhaas (A)   Feldhase (G)
Frotter des lièvres (F)   uNogwaja (Z)

The scrub hare is often seen on night drives or sunning itself during early mornings. It favours densely wooded areas with shrub cover and grazes on leaves, stems and green grass rhizomes.

The huge ears help with thermo-regulation. They are richly supplied with blood and help to dissipate heat when it is hot by exposing a large surface area to a cooling breeze. When it is cold, the hare sunbathes in the mornings to warm the blood. Its white belly and larger size distinguish it from the very similar Cape hare.

Active: (☼) ☾
Snout to tail end: 55cm
Mass: 2kg
Social structure: single, occasionally in pairs
Collective noun: a drove, husk, kindle, trace or down of hares
Gestation: 42 days (1.4 months)
Life expectancy: approximately 5 – 6 years
Enemies: many large predators, large raptors and snakes

White-tailed Mongoose
(Ichneumia albicauda)

Witstertmuishond (A)

Weißschwanzmanguste (G)

Mangouste à queue blanc (F)

gQalashu (Z)

This large mongoose is a typical eastern bushveld species and is mostly seen alone and at night. It prefers areas with good cover and close to water. The hair on the hindquarters is longer than the hair covering the front of the body. The bushy tail appears white with longer hair at the base, getting shorter towards the tip.

It is often seen in the spotlight after eight at night, with its white tail standing out, crossing the road or foraging in the undergrowth. When it is cornered or suspects danger, it freezes and lifts its tail and body hair to appear bigger. Although it can run fast over short distances, it depends on stink glands as a deterrent. It feeds on insects, preferably termites, but also takes frogs, mice, snakes and fruit.

Active: ☾

Snout to tail end: 110cm

Mass: ♂ 4.49kg ♀ 4.14kg

Social structure: solitary

Collective noun: a business of mongooses

Gestation: unknown

Life expectancy: approximately 12 years

Tawny Eagle

Bateleur

The giants and the killers

Saddle-billed Stork

African Fish Eagle

Southern Ground Hornbill

Kori Bustard

The giants and the killers

Common Ostrich

Secretarybird

Lilac-breasted Roller

African Hoopoe

Common bushveld birds

Cape Glossy Starling

Red-billed Hornbill 97

Crested Barbet

Common bushveld birds

Dark-capped Bulbul

Red-billed Oxpecker

African Darter

Birds of specific habitats

Collared Sunbird

Southern Masked Weaver

Southern Carmine Bee-eater

White-fronted Bee-eater

European Nightjar

Spotted Eagle Owl

Birds of the night

the ultimate african safari

Stretching across 13 000 hectares of African wilderness, towards the renowned Kruger National Park, lies a sanctuary of magnificent beauty and abundant wildlife. Kapama Private Game Reserve is one of South Africa's most prestigious wildlife destinations and is home to the Big Five – lion, leopard, elephant, buffalo and rhinoceros – as well as a myriad of other animals and birds.

Offering an authentic African safari experience, Kapama embodies a range of stylish accommodation across four sophisticated bush camps and lodges. Each one is meticulously positioned within this enormous wildlife sanctuary to ensure secluded and private accommodation options for every preference. The aesthetic of the architecture and décor is inspired by surrounding nature and carefully refined by creative interior designers.

Food is a focus during any stay at Kapama, with trained chefs combining flair and imagination to present inspired culinary masterpieces each day. Whilst the kitchens are the chefs' domains, Kapama's trackers and guides claim the bush as their territory. Their intimate knowledge brings game drives to life and ensures fascinating encounters with the prolific wildlife.

Kapama's close proximity to Eastgate Airport ensures swift transfers in open game viewing vehicles to Kapama's four lodges.

PRIVATE GAME RESERVE

modern charm

Set on the banks of the perennial Klaserie River, Kapama Karula means 'place of peace' in the local tribal language. This spectacular camp teems with wildlife and countless birds attracted to the glistening river water.

Exquisite large superior suites are positioned along the riverbank or tucked into the surrounding riverine bushveld, each one in its own private paradise. The natural décor tones and textures throughout the lodge reflect the understated essence and style of Kapama Karula, and this extends to the en suite facilities too. Elegant décor is contemporary-chic and combines bleached woods and richly textured fabrics to ensure the ultimate in guest comfort. All suites are fully air-conditioned.

Whilst Kapama Karula suites are spacious, they blend seamlessly into their surroundings and give a wraparound view of the surrounding bushveld. Each suite also has its own private, heated plunge pool and viewing deck. Kapama Karula ensures the ultimate luxury safari lodge experience for discerning guests.

KAPAMA
KARULA

karula wellness centre

To find peace in paradise, look no further than the ultra-luxurious Kapama Karula Wellness Centre.

Surrounded by glass, this stunning, newly-built spa has an intimate connection with the bushveld scenery. Every aspect of the spectacular design and décor invites you to pamper yourself.

With four deluxe treatment rooms and a range of revitalising health and beauty treatments, this spa uses only the finest quality products including the South African-based Healing Earth range, Dermalogica, and Moor Spa facial products. You can choose between half-day packages, day packages and spa therapy packages.

A firm favourite is the Special Elements of Africa Treatment, the ultimate rejuvenating and relaxation experience. Lying on a heated slab, you can enjoy a full body exfoliation and the warmth of heated oils and hot stones, after which the horizontal shower-heads are opened to massage the body.

The Pinotage Bliss Experience is – as its name states – blissful. It includes a detox-vine-body-wrap, a gentle Pinotage body buff, a marula milk or moor bath and invigorating hydrotherapy. A scalp massage and a Kapama marble footprint ritual complete the experience.

How about a soothing and hydrating all-over Royal Rasul Treatment with your choice of mud or body butter application? Or, for a more exhilarating experience, try the Vichy Shower, or waterfall massage.

For a body workout, the fitness centre is equipped with state-of-the-art cardio and weight-lifting equipment from Technogym. Kapama Karula offers free Wi-Fi, so you can use your Wattbike Hub app to analyse your workout data or connect to Strava, Zwift or The Sufferfest.

After working up a sweat, taking a 10-minute visit to the steam room can help relax joints and muscles, before sliding into the ice bath to help blood circulation.

The relaxation area boasts a rectangular pool - with built-in loungers and underwater jets between each seat to rejuvenate the body – which invites you to take a refreshing plunge.

If you desire a little piece of this African haven to take home, then browse through the spa curio shop before returning to your luxurious suite feeling invigorated and relaxed.

KARULA WELLNESS CENTRE

timeless safari
under canvas

Reminiscent of a traditional old African safari camp, Kapama Buffalo Camp offers an authentic African bush experience. The camp's exclusive suites are positioned on elevated platforms and surrounded by forest canopy. There's a seasonal river below, and suites are connected to each other and the main lodge by raised wooden walkways.

Rustic elements of roaring campfires, lantern light and outdoor dining under the stars contrast with the opulent comfort of air-conditioned suites, crisp white linen and every conceivable in-suite comfort. While Buffalo Camp may look old-world, it's thoroughly modern and luxurious. Whirring overhead fans lend an air of nostalgia to Buffalo Camp, and remind discerning guests of a bygone era of African safaris into unexplored wilderness.

BUFFALO CAMP

An authentic
safari experience,
linking the traveller
to nature in
understated, yet
sophisticated,
comfort.

contemporary sophistication

Located in the extreme south of the reserve, the spectacular Kapama Southern Camp offers enticing luxury thatched suites to a handful of guests. All suites are discreetly hidden in the surrounding indigenous forest. Families are also catered for at Southern Camp, with two suites specially created for this purpose.

With sweeping views over the natural waterhole frequented by animals throughout the day, the central lodge area is a favourite place to relax. Sip your choice of cocktail on the wooden viewing deck, cool off in the rim-flow swimming pool, or relax in the elegant and welcoming guest lounge. Mouth-watering gourmet meals are served either in the main dining room or in the outside boma under a star-studded night sky.

Twice-daily game drives are highlights of the day, and skilled rangers and trackers gladly share their extensive knowledge of resident wild-life with guests. Fascinating encounters in the bush are guaranteed.

Southern Camp is located close to the Wellness Centre, so a pampering for body and mind is close at hand.

SOUTHERN CAMP

vibrant luxury

Kapama River Lodge is a feat of design, with flowing, opulently furnished public spaces and an expansive wooden deck leading to a languid rim-flow swimming pool. Beyond is an expanse of soft river sand, where atmospheric, lamp-lit dinners are enjoyed under the stars.

Blending sophisticated architecture with the natural environment, River Lodge offers stylish in-suite rooms. Guests may choose between luxury suites, spa suites or stylish executive suites. Evening meals for guests are usually enjoyed around a roaring fire outdoors, while conversation is often about accounts of the day's game viewing.

RIVER LODGE

uplift mind,
body and soul

Discerningly tucked into the African bush is a sanctuary for body and mind. Kapama's Wellness Centre is considered one of the finest safari spas in Africa and is complemented by a state-of-the-art mini gym.

Therapy rooms radiate out from the central swimming pool, which creates a sense of calm for the surrounding spa. Whilst renowned beauty and treatment products are used, specially created African therapies are also on offer. Marula Miracle Moments is the signature treatment and includes a body wrap, massage, facial and other pampering treatments. The Calabash Massage and Rasul Therapy, as well as the Kapama Pinotage Bliss and Marula Sensual Steam Treatment, are other favourites. Couples' treatments are also offered by the Wellness Centre's highly trained therapists. Always up to date with global treatments, therapists incorporate the best African pamper treatments into traditional therapies to ensure complete relaxation and renewal for body and mind. It's an indulgent way to experience a different perspective of the surrounding wilderness, and seeing game whilst enjoying a spa treatment is common.

KAPAMA WELLNESS
CENTRE

Inner beauty and strength reconnect
through indulgent and invigorating
spa treatments set against an African
panoramic vista.

unparalleled african
moments in time

With Eastgate Airport in close proximity to Kapama Private Game Reserve and daily scheduled flights there from Johannesburg's airports, safari guests can be game viewing in Kapama just hours after landing in South Africa. Open-vehicle transfers take guests from Eastgate Airport to their designated safari camp, with a game drive en route.

Guests are spoilt for accommodation choice at Kapama between the classic tented Buffalo Camp, opulent nature-inspired Southern Camp, vibrant River Lodge and the chic serenity of Kapama Karula. The game viewing is thrilling across the reserve and Kapama's rangers and trackers are highly qualified and competent to interpret the sights, sounds and smells of the African bushveld. Guided bush walks are an additional offering, with the guide sharing fascinating insights into the unique ecosystem on the reserve.

For romantics and guests simply wanting to experience the wilderness without walls, a sleep-out experience on Kapama is magical. The couple spends the night sleeping on a purpose-built platform, surrounded by wilderness. An oversized four-poster bed, dressed in crisp white linen and swathed in clouds of mosquito netting, awaits them – along with an intimate dinner served on the platform. A full, luxury bathroom is located under the platform, which is completely animal-proof. This magical African experience ensures an indelible, enchanting memory of Kapama.

DEFINING AFRICA

past and present

Kapama's story is intimately entwined with the Roode family. In 1986, they bought a farm in the area for cattle grazing, but it soon became evident that cattle wouldn't survive the predators and disease there.

What followed is an epic tale of one family who recognised that the land really belongs to the wild animals of Africa – and that they are mere caretakers.

The Roode family acquired more land and tore down fences between their properties to create one extensive private game reserve, replete with Africa's big and small game. Safari ecotourism served the dual goals of giving refuge to endangered wildlife and creating jobs for the local people.

The name Kapama was adopted for the ever-expanding reserve, and named for the river that runs through it. Today, the Roode family continues to implement the vision of patriarch Johann, who passed away tragically in 2002. His wife Lente and children Bernard and Adine together manage different aspects of Kapama and have transformed it into one of Africa's leading ecotourism destinations – renowned the world over for its abundant wildlife, sound environmental practices and magnificent safari lodges, each with unique atmosphere and offerings. It is this combination, too, that ensures Kapama's future as a benchmark safari and eco-destination for nature and wildlife lovers.

KAPAMA'S HISTORY

get the most from your game drive

The best time of day

The early morning and late afternoon trigger all kinds of activities in the African bush. This is when many animals are most active – the transition from dark to light finds nocturnal animals scurrying to their daytime hiding places, leopards doing their last rounds, hyena cubs playing outside their den and lions finishing off their night-time kill. Diurnal animals leave their sleeping places, sun and groom themselves or each other, and start foraging. At dusk, diurnal animals go to rest and the nocturnal ones appear.

Drives during the middle of the day are often disappointing. Many animals are resting in the shade of trees, ruminants are chewing the cud and predators are often sleeping, lying flat and therefore not easily seen.

Some animals, however, remain active during the entire day. Bulk herbivores such as elephants continue grazing or browsing, and baboons and monkeys forage all day, often in trees, or simply sit in groups socialising and interacting with one another. Predators that are sometimes active during the heat of the day are cheetah, wild dog and some of the mongooses.

Look and listen

e alert and always expect the unexpected. Look deep into the ush, have patience and watch for movement – the flick of an ear or whisk of a tail. Camouflage is vital for survival in the bush and colours nd shapes blend perfectly into their surroundings. Listen for telltale ounds and alarm calls of animals and birds. The 'alert' posture of ntelope is another sure sign that they suspect danger.

Where to look

Notice different habitats and know what to expect in which places. ome animals have a very specific habitat preference. Lions can be xpected in almost all habitats while leopards will never go far from over. Primates depend on trees for food and safety, and hippos eed water deep enough to submerge their bodies. Klipspringers ve only on rocky outcrops, but grazers are often found in herds in he open where they feed on different kinds and heights of grasses. rowsers tend to be solitary or in small groups. They feed at differ-nt heights and from different kinds of plants.

Binoculars

inoculars are not essential, but will enhance your enjoyment during ame drives. A good pair of binoculars will focus sharply both on ear and distant objects, show only one image when viewing, and ave coated lenses to reduce the amount of light loss as it passes hrough the optical system.

  Binoculars have two specifying numbers, e.g. 7×50. The first umber indicates the power of magnification and the second the iameter in millimetres of the objective lens (the big end of the bin-culars). The most suitable binoculars are those with a magnification power of between seven and ten. The higher the power, the greater the magnification, but the steadier your hands should be.

The larger the objective lens, the more light it transmits, increasing brightness of the image, but the field of view becomes smaller and the binoculars heavier. Favourite game viewing binoculars are 7 x 35 and 8 x 32.

Photography

Take memories back home. Digital cameras are easy to use. Make sure you get a sharp photograph by setting the ISO to about 400. To avoid camera shake, try to keep the shutter speed faster than the length of the lens, i.e. if you are using a 100mm lens, set the ISO and f-stop so that the shutter speed is 1/125 per second or faster.

It is not always possible to get very close to animals, and telephoto lenses are therefore very useful. The most practical lens is anything between 100mm and 400mm. The best light is just after sunrise and just before sunset. Try to keep the sun behind you to eliminate shadows on the animal. When the light is bad, use a flash. If the flash is not strong enough to light the animal, increase your ISO setting to about 800 ISO. The most important rule in photography is: Look first. Then photograph.

Tracks

Animals are not always where one wants them to be, but at least they leave tracks for us to follow. Tracking spoor can be a lot of fun. The following double page illustrates the most common tracks you may encounter. Footprints left by large predators and some of the big herbivores can give a good indication of what may be lurking in the bush.

Front
13-14.5cm

Hind
12-15cm

Lion

Front
8-10cm

Hind
9-10cm

Leopard

Front
±30cm

Hind
±30cm

White Rhino

Front
±24cm

Hind
±23cm

Black Rhino

Front
±50cm

Hind
±50cm

Elephant

Front
±12cm

Hind
±12cm

Buffalo

Front
±10.5cm

Hind
±11.5cm

Cheetah

Front
±9cm

Hind
±8cm

African Wild Dog

Front
±26cm

Hind
±24cm

Hippopotamus

Front
±11cm

Hind
±10.5cm

Spotted Hyena

Front
±20cm

Hind
±19cm

Giraffe

Front
±8cm

Hind
±15cm

Baboon

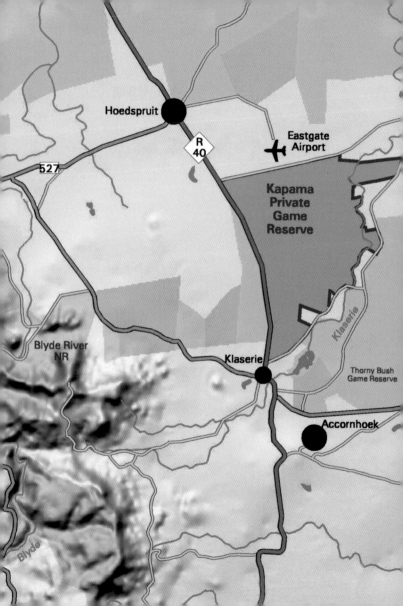

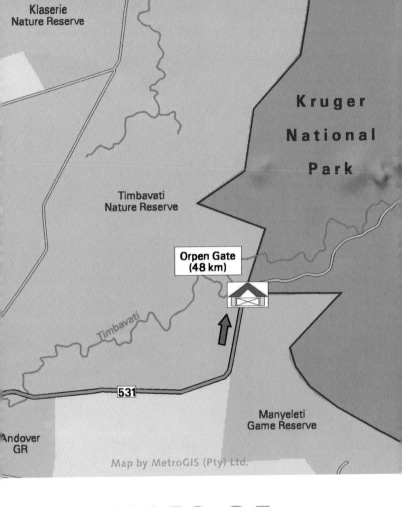

MAPS OF
KAPAMA

Eastgate
Airport

Camp
Jabulani

Kapama
River Lodge

Kapama Main
Entrance

Kapama
Karula

Southern
Camp

Buffalo
Camp

Hoedspruit
Endangered
Species Centre

Kapama
PRIVATE GAME RESERVE

Kapama Game Reserve stretches from the R40 in the west to the Thornybush boundary in the east, and from the Eastgate Airport road in the north to the Klaserie Dam in the south. The Klaserie River is one of a few rivers flowing through the reserve and is a favoured hunting ground for leopard. Kapama is a Big Five reserve with abundant wildlife. The natural environment and sweetveld ecosystem affords guests the opportunity to experience encounters with diverse wildlife that traditionally roam this area.

index

Mammals

Birds

Reptiles

Information on Kapama Game Reserve

ISBN: 978-0-620-43861-2

Seventh edition: 2017

Special edition for Kapama Private Game Reserve

Published by HPH Publishing

50a Sixth Street

Linden, 2195

E-mail: info@hphpublishing.co.za

Website: www.hphpublishing.co.za

Tel: +27 86 171 0327

First published in 2007

Copyright © HPH Publishing

Photography by

Heinrich van den Berg

Philip & Ingrid van den Berg

Except p 71 and p 87 © Nigel Dennis, Africa Imagery

Tracks by Christeen Grant

Edited by John Deane, Emma Mullen and Gillian Paizes

Design, typesetting and reproduction by

Heinrich van den Berg

Printed in China